Go as a pilgrim to the great mountains
And meet there with the spirits of the winds.
See fluted snow ridges
And snow-spume blown like smoke into trailing banner clouds.
Feel the awful presence of the creative forces
And wonder at the beauty and power of nature.
See a sunrise and a sunset, a moon rise and a moon set,
And then be at peace with yourself,
Your fellow men and creatures everywhere.

A porter pauses in a high mountain pass to catch breath and whistle for a wind. He rests his large carrying basket on his 'third leg' or 'tekuwa', a T-shaped piece of wood carried also as a walking stick that slots in beneath the basket and takes its weight from the porter's shoulders when at rest.

THE MOUNTAIN KINGDOM

The Homeland

NEPAL, THE HOME OF THE GURKHAS, lies between the great alluvial plains of India and the cold plateaux and wind-seared tablelands of Tibet. Apart from southern fringe-lands and small interior basins such as the Valley of Kathmandu that represent former lake sites, there is no flat land in Nepal. The Kingdom is one of high mountains and great rivers and is the product of powerful earth movements and the violent and relentless forces of nature.

From the air or to a person standing in a high mountain pass, the Kingdom presents itself as a series of billowing mountain ridges capped by the eternal snows of Himalayan peaks. Each mountain ridge represents a day's march for a heavily laden man: one long uphill to a cold, mossy pass and then a steep descent to a surging river, so deeply slotted into the landscape that the traveller can hear the roar of the waters long before he can see the river itself. The land is criss-crossed by mountain tracks where generations of mountain men have moved as traders, warriors, yeomen hill farmers or to tend flocks on high pastures. The mountain ridge routes lead to small sacred lakes — sites of pilgrimage set high in the mountains where the air is pure.

A traveller will be struck by the cultural landscapes of Nepal. The lower elevations of the mountain slopes, from the river terraces up to the upper levels where rice cultivation is still possible, are peopled by Hindu rice farmers. Above these levels, where low temperatures make rice cultivation impossible and where only the potato and very hardy mountain cereals grow, can be found Buddhist people who love the cold of the upper reaches of the mountains and who deck out their landscape with fluttering prayer flags that pull in the winds in even the highest passes.

Life in the mountains is very finely balanced. A late monsoon, and drought stalks the land; a violent hail storm and the maize crop will be battered flat; a torrent of monsoon rain and a landslide can remove a whole community; the terror of fire, out of control amongst the thatch covered homesteads, and life literally comes to an end as a family's shelter, hearth-place, implements, seed store and possessions are destroyed. By natural selection, only the fittest animals survive and birds of prey, wolves, bears, jackals and other marauders stalk the young of upland pens.

Left: 'Namaste!' ('Greetings to you!') — a salutation both of welcome and of departure, made here by a Gurung mother to a stranger visiting her mountain home. She is decked out in all her finery and her tartan shawl will have been sent to her by a son serving in a Gurkha Regiment far from Nepal.
Right: The Mountain Kingdom is a Hindu one but the cultural landscapes are diverse. Buddhism is found in the northern reaches of the Kingdom and also above certain elevations nearly everywhere. In the picture, tall Buddhist prayer flags pull gently in the wind and frame the summits of the giant mountain Dhaulagiri in W. Nepal.

Wherever one walks in Nepal it is nearly always against a backdrop of towering mountain peaks. From dawn to dusk the mountains are there for the walker to behold. North-east from Kathmandu is the Khumbhakarna Massif with the great node of Everest, Lhotse and Nuptse at its centre and with the incredibly beautiful summits of Kantega, Ama Dablam and Tamserku standing round the Thyangboche Lamasery, famed stopping-place on the route to Everest, where purple-robed monks and yak caravans intermingle in a brilliant landscape cradled by these giant mountains. The Himalayas, dangerous yet compelling, attract to Nepal those who seek challenge, stimulation and fulfilment in adventure high on mountain peaks.

The Splendour of the Mountains

After meeting the people of Nepal it is seeing and experiencing the mountains that make a visit memorable and worthwhile. On a northern route the mountains are always with you and one never grows tired of just looking at them, staggered by their physical beauty. No camera could ever capture adequately the glory of the dying sun as it sinks behind Dhaulagiri and throws its last rays eastwards colouring the snows of Annapurna pink and then a deep blood-red, unearthly and unbelievably beautiful. One has to be there, alone on the mountainside, to appreciate what is happening and watch as the summits of Gauri Sankar and Rowaling Himal lose their colours and merge into the night sky over the Himalayas. One has to view at firsthand the jet stream winds tearing at the summits of the mountains, trailing off streaming banner clouds as they scourge the fluted snow ridges and rounded cornices of snow.

In the silent splendour of the Himalayan dawn, the light comes back into the world and flushes pink on the pure snow of fish-tailed Machhapuchhare and in the soft snow in the courtyard of the Thyanboche Lamasery, prayer flags hang limp from their poles and the snows of Kwangde and Kantega are dark and hushed in the predawn light. In the first full light of day and from then on, the snows are a dazzling, triumphant white, and all tiredness, coldness and hunger are forgotten as one gazes at the beauty of Makalu and the wonder of its wind-whipped, wind-fluted, wind-tormented snows.

Above: The village of Tatopani, a wayside resting-place of hot springs and whitewashed homesteads on the Kali Gandaki River, W. Nepal. The Kali Gandaki has cut a mighty trench between the summits of Dhaulagiri to the west and Annapurna to the east and this trench is the deepest on the land surface of planet earth. The Nilgiris rise to the north.
Right: The village of Braga near the headwaters of the Marsyandi River, W. Nepal. The houses are clustered together for ease of defence and the flat roofs are used as sun traps where grains are dried and stored and where people meet to talk and socialize. The village lies in the rain shadow of the Annapurna massif, trees are scarce and erosion, deep and spectacular.

Previous page: Morning light, mists and reflections on the waters of Begnas Tal, W. Nepal. The early sun gives warmth to the ochre walls of the homesteads and to the north the winter snows reach far down the flanks of the Himalayas. The central peak is that of Machhapuchhare, flanked by the more distant Annapurna massifs.

Above: The beehive-like clusters of round houses of the village of Pamdur, set amidst fields of winter wheat, W. Nepal. These round houses are found only in certain parts of W. Nepal. Like all mountain homes they have thick rubble-filled walls that are warm and snug in winter yet cool and places of shelter from hot suns. Construction detail can be seen in the picture on the right.

Himalayan mountain scenery is fashioned first by wind and ice. The upper snow ridges are fluted by the wind and wind builds up and smooths the delicate cornices of the summit peaks. It is snow, accumulated and pressed into ice that forms the glaciers that carve out the upper Himalayan valleys and grind ridge lines until only narrow razor-back arêtes remain. The upper ice fields also eat back into mountain peaks from all sides to form pyramidal horns and the hanging snowfields on these horns spawn huge powdered avalanches that, triggered off by earth movements or by thaw, descend through thousands of feet with a destructive violence and explosive power that is awesome to behold. Nobody who has listened to the roar of a large airborne avalanche or experienced the awful chill and suffocating vacuum in the lee of such an avalanche can be anything but awestruck at the enormity of nature's power in the Himalayas.

When the temperature rises sufficiently, ice becomes water that seeps into crack and cranny there to refreeze and expand and force the rocks apart. Freeze-thaw shatters the mountain rocks and sends rock detritus tumbling down onto the chaos of the grinding, crushing blocks of glacier ice below.

The Great Rivers

When the high snow fields and glaciers melt, streams are born and small rivers flow from glacier snouts. Streams coalesce, gather force and become rivers that continue to erode the land as they flow south to a final union in the waters of the Ganges. The great rivers of Nepal, cradled by the mountains and flowing north to south, have kept pace with the Himalayas rising across their courses by cutting gorges deep into the mountains that wrinkled up across their lines of flow. The tributaries of the Sapt Kosi, the Kali Gandaki and the Karnali have all cut deep gorges through Himalayan ramparts.

The rivers are both constructive and destructive. It is the rivers that help make the rice culture of Nepal possible by flooding and laying down fertile silt on river terraces and by bringing water to the thousands of feet of

Left: A bridge of heavy logs cantilevered out over the headwaters of the Tamur River, E. Nepal. The bridge may not survive the next wet monsoon when rain and glacial melt waters will cause the Tamur to rise spectacularly and surge down its course at great speed.
Right: The beautiful colours of the winter landscape of the Bheri Valley, W. Nepal. The villages seek the better soils near the river or cling, step-like, to steep mountain sides.

Top: Tukucha Peak, W. Nepal. The morning sun lights up the mist-shrouded mountain while the coniferous trees of the lower slopes are still in deep shadow.
Above: Patch-fields of potatoes, barley and rye grow green near Namche Bazaar where Sherpa farmers have managed to cultivate small pockets of soil set in an otherwise harsh landscape of rock and boulders.

Top (right): Delicate conifer branches frame the summit of Kantega and its great ice walls. Kantega is one of the giant peaks passed by mountaineers on their way to Mount Everest.
Right: The Thyanboche Lamasery, famed stopping-place on the route to Everest. The main temple is in the centre and the homes of purple-robed Buddhist monks lie clustered round it.

layered terracing that cling, step-like, to the mountain sides of Nepal. Yet, these same life-giving streams and rivers become surges of glacial melt and rain water at the height of the wet monsoon and they then tear at the landscape, powerfully eroding and undercutting their banks, the terraces and the paddy fields above to cause landslides, destruction of villages and death. Ruthless surges of destruction by rivers undo the work of decades in a few hours.

The rivers of Nepal have a thousand moods that stagger the imagination. Here the waters lie emerald green in deep pools behind protective rock bastions; there the waters are the browns of a trout stream where they shallow over fords. Here the waters run smooth and deep; there an angry surge of melt water boils and foams where a rock impedes its flow. The Dudh Kosi is so named from the colour of its water, milky white when laden with glacier dust and silt. The Bheri Khola is cobalt blue as the waters are free of silt and reflect the blue Himalayan sky. Shallow and fordable in the dry season, the same rivers in the wet monsoon become powerful vortices that sweep with great destructive force towards the plains of India.

Rivers are barriers to the movement of men and must be crossed. In Nepal, crossings can be by steel suspension bridges built in the late nineteenth century by Scottish engineers or by crazy, plank-rotten stepways suspended from wire handrails. Here a switchback bridge built out of bent bamboo is crazily warped, and, sagging, spans a surging river branch; there some local engineer has carefully cantilevered out some massive tree-planks across the river below his village.

Where bridges have been beyond the capability of man, an expert class of ferrymen ply their dugout ferryboats across the rivers using skilled judgement, the force of the current and large steering paddles to get their passengers unharmed and dry to a far bank. No Gurkha enters such a dugout without blessing the boat and the spirits of the waters and praying for a safe ferry to the far side. A cord of special string, priest-blessed and worn next to the skin may save the wearer from

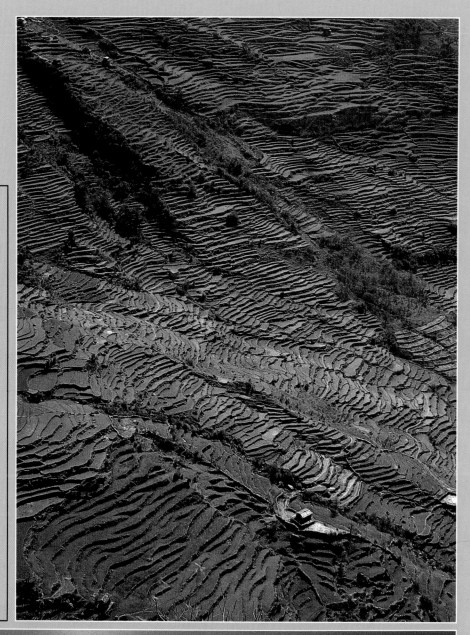

Right: The terraced mountain slopes of the Myangdi Valley, W. Nepal. Much energy is required not only to build and maintain the terraces but to ensure that the life-giving irrigation waters can and do trickle from terrace to terrace down through thousands of feet. The homestead gives the scale.

Left: The stark pyramidal horn of Machhapuchhare dominates this rustic spring scene.

Below: The sun breaks through to burn up the night mists from the floor of the Lukum Valley in central W. Nepal.

Left: Mountaineers have sought stimulation and fulfilment high on mountain peaks in the Himalayas down the decades. Purna-bahadur Mall of the Gurkha Independent Parachute Company climbed on Annapurna I with the author in 1970.
Far Left: The morning sun begins to invade the small township of Dingla, E. Nepal.

Above: The sun lights up Ghumte Pahar in W. Nepal as the final traces of morning mist clear its flanks. *Opposite:* Deep morning shadows cap the dense village of Taka in central W. Nepal.

high priority in the future economic development of Nepal. The forests must be replanted and allowed to mature; on maturity, they must be cropped scientifically and not cut and burned and munched into obscurity again. The basic problem is that to see at night, to cook a meal, have hot water or to be warm, the people of Nepal must have a fire: there is no alternative fuel to wood, hence the dilemma.

Flowers are widely used as a decorative medium, yet behind the seemingly innocent desire for decoration, there lies a religious significance, a desire to appease, thank and be at one with the gods. Thus, in the same way that bridges are decorated so also are the shrines and the resting places, the water pitchers and the baskets that carry the food, each one decorated with a small garland of flowers. Every waterhole, crossing place, mountain peak and oddly-shaped rock outcrop has its own guardian spirit that is appeased by the simple act of placing some mountain flowers near its abode in the water or on the mountainside, as the case may be.

Mountain Men

The Gurkhas are the products of a hard environment and the Mountain Kingdom already described is their homeland. The mountains and the rivers and the monsoon climate condition the Gurkha's way of life and the majority are subsistence farmers living by the toil of their hands, by their hardiness and by their resilience and durability. They know that to live comfortably even at subsistence level, they must expend great physical effort to build their rice terraces and then to repair, plough and cultivate them.

They can be seen as tiny children alone in the landscape, sticks clutched in small hands, beating the flanks of large, lumbering water buffaloes tethered out to graze. They grow up the equal of each other and of any task set them. Men are equals because they have suffered and survived the same hard environment as equals, each on his own. The thought that one man is better than another is quite foreign to Gurkha philosophy. They are the equal of the world and ask only their khukuris and other agricultural implements

drowning if the ferry should capsize. The suspension cables of bridges are also blessed and are decorated with flowers by travellers before they step out onto the swaying planks to grip the rails with fear-whitened hands.

Trees and Flowers

Trees are so scarce in Nepal that one always stands and admires them when one comes across them in numbers and because they are so beautiful. The dark-green gloss of the thick-leaved rhododendron trees stands in marked contrast to the shimmering greens of the new fir trees. In the cool, clean moss forests of the higher mountain slopes, where orchids and delicate tree-ferns grow in profusion, there, in haunts unknown to man, long-tailed birds and tufted green woodpeckers flit silently from branch to branch in silent courtship.

It is the tragedy of Nepal today that her forests have been so badly devastated. Goats and man between them have ruined the natural climax tree cover of Nepal and every year landslides take a terrible toll of human life, sweeping entire communities into the surging waters of the rivers during the wet monsoon. Reafforestation must be given a

Above: The winter Himalayan jet stream tearing at the summit of Annapurna I. An instrument placed by a mountaineer attempts to record wind speeds.
Right: Cold, arid 'moonscape' topography, near Muktinath, pilgrimage centre en route to the cold plateaux of Mustang and Tibet. There is no tree cover and the river has deeply eroded its bed and scarred the landscape.
Opposite: The splendour of the early morning sun on the snows of Machhapuchhare, the sacred mountain that dominates the Pokhara Valley. The settlements are on the flats of former lake sites now deeply incised by swift tributaries of the Seti River.

to tackle their difficult environment. They build their own homes and live in self-sufficient family units. What they require, they construct; what they eat, they produce themselves. They understand the cycle of life and of the seasons and the complete life spans of the Gurkhas and their daily tasks are determined by the rising of the sun, by sudden hail, by fire, by luck (or fate?) and by the arrival or failure of monsoon rains.

A Gurkha boy thus grows towards manhood as a sturdy, independent, self-sufficient and capable being, inured to privation and hardship and capable of finding his own way in the world and of

meeting all his wants by means of his own bodily labour. They are proud of themselves, their virility and of their families and they can smile at the world and laugh easily at the thought that life could ever get them down. With their black hair spiky from sweat and creased by the headbands of their heavy baskets, they reach the mountain pass in the early dawn. Here they pause to sing because it is dawn and they are alive and because, having reached the pass, there will be a pause there before the long descent on the other side. Life is that pleasurable and that simple and the products of the mountains of this Kingdom of Nepal are these energetic, enduring people who are so generous, so brave and so full of fortitude.

Above: Dawn and the sun-flushed summit of Dhaulagiri, taken from Shepherd's Camp en route to the Annapurna I Base Camp.

Below: Life can be fragile in the Mountain Kingdom. Here a few homesteads have found lodgement on a small terrace stuck to a steep mountain side.

Above: The flanking glaciers of Dhaulagiri seem to threaten the small temple and houses of the village of Debi that nestles at the foot of this giant mountain. The large, substantial homesteads are those of the Thakali people. The flat roofs are used for drying grain and as meeting places and access is by the notched ladders, cut from forest trees. The interiors have cattle stalls on the ground floor and people live in large rooms above the stalls. The windows may have glass, an innovation amongst the hill tribes.

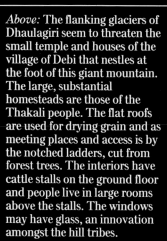

THE YEARLY CYCLE

The Wet Monsoon — The Miracle of Rice Culture

NEPAL HAS A MONSOON CLIMATE. From early June until late September, due to great overheating in the plains of India, the monsoon winds, moisture-laden, are sucked up the Ganges Valley from the Bay of Bengal and they lash the Mountain Kingdom with heavy and incessant rain. On a landscape devoid of trees either to break the force of the rain or help stabilize the soils, these rains run off quickly to the rivers, causing them to swell and surge down their courses. Days are overcast and it can rain for a week without let up. The rains create havoc by causing landslides as the mountain soils and the paddy fields, clogged with moisture, become overheavy and slip and slump towards the swelling waters of the rivers.

The rains do, however, make the rice culture of Nepal possible. The rains sweep the mountains clean of their thin soils and deposit these soils on mountain and river terraces. Here, on the steep mountain slopes of Nepal, the Gurkhas take part with nature in the miracle of wet rice cultivation. It is a time of maximum activity on the land; there is no time for religion or schooling now as family units tend to the preparation of their paddy lands, the men ploughing the flooded soils and the women and children planting out the delicate rice seedlings. Rice seedlings require water moving slowly past their roots while they are growing and the rice seeds are swelling and so on steep mountain sides peasant farmers have carefully graded the land and the terraces so that the irrigation waters are continually in motion from the topmost terraces where the stream or small river is first tapped, down through thousands of feet of terracing to the major river below.

The containing wall of each paddy field has an inlet and outlet where the waters enter and depart and each Gurkha farmer is dependent that the neighbour immediately above will work in harmony with the rest of the vast mountain slope and let the waters trickle down. Stagnant water would lead to salt accumulation, sour paddy lands and sterile rice seedlings. Generations have worked to construct and maintain with endless repair work the rice terraces of Nepal and it is with awe that a traveller looks upon the human effort involved in a mountain slope stepped through thousands of feet by human hands.

By October, the waters are draining off the terraces and the rice is ripening fast. November and December see the hill farmers busy with cutting and threshing the rice crop

and faced with the back-breaking work of hauling both rice seed and rice straw up many hundreds of feet from their paddy fields to their homesteads. Here, the life-sustaining rice seed is carefully stored in rodent-proof containers in household attics and the straw carefully piled into small outhouses or stacked in courtyards. Throughout the coming twelve months, the mother of the house will carefully ration out the rice seed as food and watch the levels in the rice containers to ensure that the family will not go riceless before the next year's crop is harvested and brought in.

Below: In the dry season and particularly for the October Hindu festival of Dasain, swings are built for all to enjoy. Here the author's porters enjoy themselves on a large swing at Hang Pang, E. Nepal. Bets are made to see who can swing highest, and falls and broken bones are not unknown!

Opposite: Nepal is a land of rugged scenery sculpted by ice and powerful rivers. Throughout the cycle of the seasons, however, are scenes of great tranquility and subtle beauty. In the picture, it is spring in a mountain forest above Jajarkot in W. Nepal and the early sun bathes the delicate foliage of the trees with gentle light.

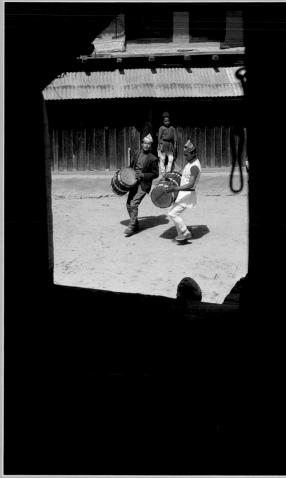

The dry monsoon is a time for marriages and people turn to song and dance.

Left and above: Limbu drummers play at a courtyard wedding. The large drums are made from bark and are decorated with red mountain rhododendrons. The playing surfaces (both ends of the drums) are of hide and are lovingly preserved and prepared before each performance. *Bottom left and below:* Gurung drummers and dancers perform a dance of welcome. All performers are plied with food and drink and are rewarded with rice or small cash offerings.

Above: A Limbu harvest courtship dance: one youth tugs shyly at the shawl of a fancied girl. *Left:* A male dancer, dressed to dance a female role. (Beyond puberty, girls generally relinquish dancing in public.) *Below:* A Limbu bridesmaid at Wasum, E. Nepal.

Life During The Rains

The Gurkhas thus live life cycles closely controlled and conditioned by the monsoon climate of their Mountain Kingdom. During the wet monsoon they are out in the teeming rain, crossing the leech infested mountain slopes to their paddy fields. There, with a team of buffaloes or bullocks they wrestle their metal-pointed ploughs through the flooded soils of the small fields, fighting the lumbering animals and the heavy plough round the contours until the soils are well and truly stirred up to the porridge-like consistency of swamp soils.

At night, often after dark, they return home to wash in stream water and change their homespun garments by the side of the open fire burning in a shallow pit in the floor of their single-roomed homes. As they change, their women folk cook the main evening meal of rice which is eaten by the light and the warmth of this open fire. After the meal the fire flares again and the males chatter by the light, snug now within the thick, rubble-filled walls of their homes and with the day's work at an end. Soon the fire dies and the household sleeps on rough sleeping platforms next to the walls. Life is close and intimate and once the light of the fire has died down to a red glow, nobody cares.

Throughout the wet monsoon there is always the fear that a landslide will remove a family's house and paddy soils. In the interior of a Gurkha household during the wet monsoon when the rain is lashing the mountain slopes, parents listen to nature while children sleep. The next morning well before it is daylight and while the men and children sleep on, the women are up and the noises of heavy hand-worked stones grinding grain into flour and of rice seed being pounded under heavy blows of a foot-worked metal-pointed beam, sound throughout quiet houses and courtyards. As the cocks begin to crow, the men and the youths are up and having partaken only of some tea or rice beer with a piece of unleavened bread, they collect the animals and the ploughs and leave for the fields once more. As they plough, they look towards the end of the rains when the weeding and the hoeing of the rice seedlings will be over and when they can relax and watch the rice fields ripen under a hot sun.

Above: A family oil press. The weighted upright is walked round to squeeze out the oil from the oil seeds. Sugarcane may be similarly treated. *Below:* Fields of mustard and of winter wheat. The fields and buildings are part of the Hindu cultural landscape. Higher up and in the colder clime of the pass can be seen the white buildings and prayer flags of the Buddhist cultural landscape.

Facets of the yearly cycle: *(Above)* A set of flooded rice terraces below Bhojpur, E. Nepal. *(Right)* Gurung women spin and weave in the courtyard of their home at Siklis, W. Nepal. *(Below)* Mustard, honeysuckle and grey thatch.

Right: A Rai girl at the village water point. If no natural water source is at hand, water is brought from afar by sections of bamboo used to channel the water to the chosen site. The final spout is generally made of hard, durable wood as in the picture. *Below:* The day sun lightens the interior of a village home to show baskets full of seed (the next year's crop) and also the food store of pumpkins and gourds, carefully kept to ward off starvation should the main rice and grain crops fail for any reason. *Bottom right:* A Magar granny carrying a load and spinning wool onto a spindle as she goes about her tasks.

Above: Water-collecting is generally a woman's task and a happy Rai girl is seen with a traditional metal water pot on her hip. As is the custom, family wealth is kept in the form of gold and worn as jewellery by the women. *Left:* A shy young Limbu girl amongst her maize crop.

Below: Rai elder (on right of picture with white parchment in his hands) of Tap Khola, E. Nepal addresses a winter gathering on village matters such as tithes or the communal labour required to repair a bridge or stretch of road. The people will have been summoned by the village crier calling from a local vantage point.

The Dry Monsoon — A Time of Joy

The dry monsoon in Nepal completes the year and the life cycle in the mountains. The dry monsoon covers the greater part of the year and lasts from October until the rains begin again. The dry monsoon thus covers autumn, winter and spring and it is a time of great beauty in the Himalayas with azure blue skies and a dust free atmosphere. In April and May come sharp thunder and rain storms that are the forerunners of the wet monsoon and they herald the change of spring into summer. Overheating may at times cause heavy convectional showers and always there is the danger that rain will fall as hail and batter down the swelling maize cobs. Such violent hail storms can mean famine to any family short on rice and looking to the maize crop for food.

The dry monsoon is a time of grain crop cultivation and the Gurkhas produce crops of rye, barley, wheat and maize. No land is left unused and even the level tops of the rice terrace walls are planted out with lentils and other pulses. Near the homesteads are the vegetable gardens where marrows, pumpkins, chillies and green vegetables are grown and here also will be the banana, mango, orange and other fruit trees that a family owns.

The autumn and winter months are joyous ones on the land. The rice crop has been gathered in and the household granaries are full. The autumn fruits are on the trees and sweet oranges are hanging in clusters from sagging branches. The winter grain crops are in the ground and the sun is shining. It is a time of plenty and the Gurkhas turn again from the toil of mountain rice culture back to religion and to thank their gods in festivals of harvest thanksgiving. As Hindus or Buddhists they bring simple offerings of food and produce from their land and offer them gratefully to their gods as acts of faith that life will go on and that the following year's monsoon will not fail.

Above: The plough, an essential instrument amongst the subsistence farmers of Nepal, seen here against the ochre-coloured wall of a mountain homestead. The yoke for the oxen (cows are sacred and never used for ploughing) is on the two house struts above the plough.

Left: A pause by a sunlit Buddhist shrine in a mountain pass. The shrine here is a prayer wall and believers always keep such walls on their right as they pass them.

Above: Every village has its own family of blacksmiths and they (despite being low caste) are vital to the community they serve for it is they who forge scrap metal into the agricultural implements that all farmers must have if life is to go on. In the picture, a khukuri is beginning to take shape in the skilled hands of the artisan.

Left: A young Magar girl carries her young sister (dressed in an ornate cap) to a village wedding.

The Cycle of Life

There is much work to be done during the long dry season but it is not marked by quite the same frenzied activity that marks the onset of the monsoon rains when much work has to be accomplished in a much shorter time-span. In the dry winter, house repairing and house building are done as are repairs to fences and to retaining walls of the paddy terraces. The land has to be prepared for the wheat and other grain crops and manure has to be spread over the family fields by tethering out the animals. A village may combine its male labour to repair a bridge or stretch of road. Agricultural implements must be repaired and the dry season is a time to do business, to plan and negotiate the purchase of a further piece of choice hillside for grazing or of riverside terrace for rice cropping. There is that choice set of terraces just down from his fields that the father has always cast an eye on; would the neighbour sell now if the money could be got together somehow? Children go to school again and the young can visit local wayside bazaars. And what of the third eldest son? It is time he was married and perhaps this autumn a bride should be searched for and the marriage arranged?

Firewood is sought and stacked and men go off hunting. Once during the dry season also, with the granaries full and the trees heavy with fruit, the household males will join with other families and undertake the back-breaking trip to the plains — an economic pilgrimage to acquire the essentials of life that the mountain farmers cannot produce themselves. Small agricultural surpluses and other goods such as khukuris forged in upland smithies are carried on the backs of men and boys to the plains and loads of salt and paraffin brought back to the villages. While on the plains and buying and selling in the bazaars, it may also be possible to have a son recruited into the army. There is thus essential work to be done throughout the dry season for the continued well-being of family units, but there is time for people to participate in family and village gatherings for dance and for song that lead to relationships, courtship and marriage and so to the continuance of life.

The yearly cycle in Nepal is thus a cycle of life, of crops being planted and made to

It is dawn in the Himalayas. A small, shy boy has come down early from his mountain home and is first at the village water point. The wind is still ice-cold from the snows of the mountains but soon the sun will strengthen and warm his chilled body. He is collecting water in sections of bamboo and will carry them on a headband up the steep track to his homestead. Then he will take the family flocks out to graze and, as he sits in the sun while the animals feed, so his mind will range beyond his Mountain Kingdom to lands where Gurkhas serve for it is his wish to be a soldier one day and so a proud provider for his parents and his brothers and sisters.

grow and of the delivery of young animals in upland cattle pens. The cycle involves the entire family unit in immense effort on the land. There is man-work and woman-work and child-work and all must do their share. Near to nature, the people respect her moods and accept her challenges. They revel in the joys of autumn and mourn when a landslide destroys a human community. New life —

the birth of a young thing — is gloried in by the Gurkha; death he accepts in his own phlegmatic way. He himself is the most enduring facet of his Mountain Kingdom; it is his hardihood and labour and his ability to smile and overcome the hardships that beset him in his mountain valleys that ensure that the yearly cycle on the land does go on and that the cycle of life is maintained.

VARIED JAT AND CLAN

The Cultural Mix.

THERE IS GREAT VARIETY amongst the tribes that inhabit Nepal. These tribal differences are partly definable in terms of anthropology and of where tribes originated from and partly in terms of caste and in the positions that the tribes occupy on the strict Hindu scale of caste dominance based on occupation. The basic ethnic division of the country can be done geographically by putting the capital city Kathmandu at the centre of the realm. Any tribal groupings east of Kathmandu are then definable as having originated from the north and northeast, born out of migrations southward into Nepal of mongolian peoples moving out from the valleys and platèaux of the southern rimlands of south central Asia. Any tribal groupings west of Kathmandu are equally definable as having originated from an influx of Hindu migrants who came to Nepal from the plains of India. Nepal is a Hindu realm but all the trappings of the Buddhist faith are also evident in many parts of the Kingdom.

Eastern Warriors

East Nepal is the home of two main warrior tribes, the Rais and the Limbus and within each there are many sub-tribes or clans, each with a definite home area and tribal base. Many and complex are these Rai and Limbu tribal variations, and it is only after long conversation with a man that it becomes clear how he is related to the mainstream of Rai or Limbu life. As well as the Rais and Limbus in the east, there are also tribes of Sunwars, Tamangs and Gurungs, the latter, having originated from west of Kathmandu, came east with western armies when western warlords sacked the valley of Kathmandu in the late eighteenth century and, victorious, carved out estates for themselves and prizes for their followers from territories east of the Capital.

The Rais and Limbus are the nearest thing in Nepal to pure mongolian stock; they are small in stature, averaging 5' 3" in height, with black hair, dark eyes and wheaten complexions. They have little body or facial hair and the Gurkha soldier is almost beardless if he is of mongolian stock. The classic Limbu head is long and has a well developed bridge to the nose. The typical Rai head is small and round with practically no bridge to the nose at all. Both Rais and Limbus have almond shaped eyes due to pronounced epicanthic folding of their eyes and they all have wonderful teeth and flash white-toothed grins when happy. As there is little sweetness in the land beyond honey and sugar cane, their teeth are powerful and good as also are their constitutions: the only parts of a chicken that survive any meal are the beak and claws, every other piece of flesh and bone is solemnly munched into obscurity.

The Gurkha's body is exceptionally strong in the legs, the back and the neck and shoulders, the muscles of these parts having

Left: A Magar girl of the village of Lukum, W. Nepal. *Opposite:* A young Magar boy who approached the author's camp site full of curiosity but too shy to venture beyond the fence of his father's fields.

Varied Jat and Clan: *Clockwise from top:* Rice merchant in blue scarf; professional porter smokes in the Nepali way; ploughman of Modi Khola; tribal girl at well; herd-boys of Pasgam. *Opposite page:* A shy smile from a little Gurung girl in a wheat field near her home at Bhichuk, W. Nepal.

been powerfully developed by walking in the mountains carrying heavy loads suspended from a headband. The Gurkha's arms, as they do little more than balance any basket load, are correspondingly weak until they have been given special exercises to develop and strengthen them. Gurkhas are not naturally supple nor athletic nor are they fast runners without training because their lives have been conditioned by an environment that forces them to plod slowly up steep gradients with heavy loads, to stop and draw breath every so often and then to whistle for a wind in the pass before descending the far side, their pad-like feet and almost prehensile toes gripping the track and raising scurries of dust as they let their heavy knee muscles take the weight of the laden baskets on the downward stretches.

Western Counterparts

The main martial tribes of west Nepal are the Magars, the Gurungs, the Thapas and the Puns. Here again, there are complex subdivisions into sub-tribes and clans and into 'pure' and 'impure' groupings depending on whether or not children were born of tribal parents or from a union of a tribal male with a woman of another tribe. These western men are broader and stockier than the slimmer, slighter built mongolian strains of east Nepal and their complexions are swarthier and they grow more body and

The family priest of Dadra Gaun, W. Nepal.   Little Gurung girl of Daruwadursa, W. Nepal.

facial hair. Their eyes are less almond shaped and more open, their hair jet black and their average height has not altered from that of eastern tribes.

If the mongolian tribes are renowned as men slow to anger, but of violent temper and belligerent stance once roused, then the western tribes are perhaps men of quieter disposition, with a greater love of dancing and singing and with a greater variety of tribal music and dance patterns. All Gurkhas have dark eyes that are clear and of powerful vision and it is the eyes that do much to give the Gurkha his cheerful, open, frank and friendly countenance.

Sherpas and Thakalis

Living in north-eastern Nepal up along the frontier with Tibet are the Sherpa tribes, famed mountaineers, strict Buddhists and one of the last tribal groupings to enter Nepal from the north. The Sherpas are skilled traders and by means of their business acumen can accumulate considerable wealth. Their homes are comfortable and contain luxuries and often the trappings of modern mountaineering and trekking cooperatives. They own yak and mule caravans, were once engaged in trade with Tibet to the north for salt and today trade with the lowland bazaars of Nepal to the south for rice, sugar, tea and other luxuries. Sherpas are gay people with that glow of health that mountaineers exude and with complete unconcern for cold, heavy frosts or the threat of snow. Sherpas deck out

their landscape with all the trappings of fervent Buddhism and while every mountain top and ridge line is festooned with prayer flags pulling in the mountain winds, so every stream has a prayer wheel built on it to be kept in perpetual motion by water power.

West of Kathmandu the Sherpas are balanced by the Thakali tribes. The men-folk of these tribes are pastoralists, herding large flocks of sheep for their wool on the flanks of the western Himalayas while the women-folk run the spotlessly clean wayside stopping-places where they charm weary travellers with their hospitality, convivial company, tasty food and well run establishments. These stopping-places are often quite ephemeral, built out of plaited bamboo and thatch on dry river beds to serve the heavy winter monsoon foot traffic to the plains, but removed before the wet monsoon once again sends the rivers coursing down the entire width of their beds.

People of The Valley

The Valley of Kathmandu has a tribe of shopkeeper craftsmen of its very own. These are the Newars, the open-eyed original inhabitants of the Valley who perfected the architecture of the pagoda and who are experts at working in every medium from stone and wood to silver, brass and gold. Their internal system of caste allied to craft is a complex one and the man who moulds the clay is on a different caste plane from he who works in gold. Devout and loyal Hindus, the Newars have a temple culture smothered in erotic carvings, brilliantly painted images

Right: Firewood is searched for every day by all the people of Nepal and the search for a single load may take a whole day where forests have been ravaged. Here, a mother returns with a heavy load, expertly packed and with a cushion of mountain grass between the load and her back.
Below: A young Limbu boy of E. Nepal with a 'tongba', the traditional Limbu drinking vessel. Made of special wood and banded with metal, the vessels are filled with fermented rye and hot water, the resultant liquid being drunk via the wooden pipe or 'pipsing' that is inserted through the lid. The vessel is topped up with more hot water from time to time.

Below: A member of the professional musician caste plays his mountain violin at a wayside bazaar. *Opposite:* Red-cloaked scribe of Baglung, W. Nepal. A professional writer, he makes a living by drawing up documents for people.

and statues of Hindu mythology daubed with paint and flower-blessed daily by thousands of believing hands.

Caste Hierarchy

Spread out amongst the mountain homes and villages of the warrior castes of both east and west Nepal are other smaller and lesser tribes linked to other occupations than warring and so deemed more menial in the Hindu caste scale. If a Gurkha wants clothes made he summons a professional tailor from the Damai tribe; if he wants music at a marriage or a funeral, he calls a professional musician; should a new khukuri be required then an order is placed with a village where Kamis live, for a blacksmith there to forge the wanted blade. A tribe of ferrymen tend the river crossings on the great rivers and a tribe of potters makes the vessels that carry water and hold grain and rice beer in mountain homesteads.

The priestly tribe of Bauns are called for child-naming, marriages, horoscope reading and deaths and there are wandering minstrels, hermits, witch doctors and spirit men who fall without known tribe and caste boundaries and who visit by night to read the future from a few seeds of rice, to exorcise a ghost or return a lost spirit from the deep forests. The hierarchy of caste is real and caste boundaries deeply engrained in the social life of the Kingdom. Gurkhas in the regiments will forget and forgive caste

Left: A marvellous smile from a small Roka boy of central W. Nepal. He is still wearing his earrings and his large silver bangle is to protect him from evil and to bring him luck. He carries his mother's fire-blackened cooking pot.

Below Left: A grandmother of the small Gurung village of Bejang, W. Nepal. She has just completed the cleaning of the small deerskin to her left and set it on a frame to dry in the sun.

Below: The Gurung Jemedar (Lieutenant) of Dadra Gaun. An ex-serviceman and expert dancer, he danced in the cold mountain air for hours decked out in his colourful Nepali hat ('topi') and western-style dressing-gown. To show appreciation, onlookers approached him and tucked paper Nepali rupees just under the edge of his hat so that at the end of his dance his head was festooned in a halo of Nepali money.

Opposite: Small Magar boy with his pet cockerel.

Left: Rai farmer of Tap Khola, E. Nepal, in traditional dress of tunic, voluminous-seated trousers, cloth waistband and Nepali 'topi'. In his waistband is his khukuri. If the trousers were not voluminous, movement up and down steep mountain sides would be restricted. In W. Nepal the problem of free limb movement was overcome by adopting a kilt-like garment or 'khas', identical in concept to the Highland kilt of Scotland.

Below left: Young Bura with pellet-bow and small satchel of clay pellets, Tamangaon, W. Nepal.

Below: 'Going home.'

divisions and their military way of life is not interrupted by them, but a Gurkha in Nepal follows valley and village caste custom. A high caste will not eat with a low one nor allow the shadow of a low caste person to fall upon his food; a high caste Hindu will strip and wash before preparing his own food with his own hands; a warrior will doff his Nepalese cap, smear a wetted hand over his honest face and proceed to eat his food with minimum fuss and no further undressing.

Cultural Landscapes

Due to differences in tribal origins, cultural differences abound and are evident in the landscape. There is a Sherpa landscape characterized by the visible material objects of the Buddhist faith and by culture of the potato. A yak ploughing beside a village of whitewashed houses with slatted wooden roofs weighted down by stones is a cultural scene that could only belong to a Sherpa landscape. Prayer flags and prayer walls belong to the Sherpa culture and if they are found in other parts of Nepal then it is because the Sherpa has left his home in north-east Nepal and settled there. The men of eastern Nepal carry their loads in baskets

Left: Gurung mother of Daruwadursa, W. Nepal with a cockerel as a gift for the author. *Above:* Wayside butcher cutting meat Nepali-style, his khukuri reversed and wedged against his body as he cuts. The meat is almost always pork or goat and is sold by weight, the pieces of meat being skewered onto slivers of bamboo for ease in carrying them home.

that are larger and of a different shape from the baskets of western men. Eastern men smoke their leaf tobacco rolled in leaves; western men smoke their tobacco in small stemless clay pipes or through a water-pipe. There are only square-shaped homesteads in eastern Nepal; in parts of western Nepal a completely circular house is found. The Gurkha of east Nepal while on the trail would periodically rest his heavy basket on a special T-shaped stick that fits into a slot in the base of his basket; the western man has no such basket nor such an aid to rest his load on.

Tribal languages vary dramatically and are kept alive by the women even if the men of the martial tribes learn a lingua franca through service in the regiments. A Sherpa speaks the language of Tibet, a Limbu through his nose and a Newari the language of the large villages and townships where they have their cultural homes. The dress of east and west is different. Go to eastern Nepal and see how many men wear turbans as western men are wont to do; go west and search in vain for a man wearing the voluminous-seated trousers of the Limbus. The khukuri is one of the main agricultural

implements (turned weapon) of the eastern tribes and is replaced by the sickle as an implement and cutting tool all over western Nepal.

Common Human Qualities

Despite all these differences born out of varied ethnic backgrounds, religions and caste hierarchies, the deep human qualities of the Gurkhas are the same. They are hospitable and kind and generous by nature and they share what little they have readily and with open and meaningful hearts. What little they have is yours for the asking and in times of shortage, food and material things are shared with those who are without. They are also gentlemen and have that innate courtesy found amongst highlanders the world over. They are polite in their speech and they venerate old age and pay homage to elders and senior relatives. Parents are revered and a son bows to touch the feet of his parents who begat him. Resilient and enduring, perhaps their greatest characteristic is their innate cheerfulness in adversity and the white-toothed smile and ready friendship that they offer those who seek their company.

Left: The matriarch of Taka, W. Nepal. Her ear lobes, pierced to take jewellery, here carry small wooden plugs and the short clay pipe she has is found in most parts of W. Nepal and is smoked by both men and women. It is not found in E. Nepal where people smoke their tobacco rolled into the dry outer leaves of maize cobs.

Varied Jat and Clan: *Clockwise from top left:* Tea seller of Ilam; Magar bridesmaids of Lukum; the priest; pipe-smoker in a patched jacket in the Pass of Balangra, central W. Nepal. The pipe does not touch his lips, the smoke being drawn through the cupped hands, as in this way the pipe can be passed from person to person in a group.

THE ECONOMIC PILGRIMAGE

The Need to Travel

EVERY YEAR towards the end of September, the wet monsoon begins to ease and the sun breaks through again onto a flooded landscape where the back-breaking work of paddy planting is over for the year. The sun will now dry the land and for almost six months there will be little rain. Foodstocks and provisions in the small mountain homesteads are now low and there is little salt or paraffin left in either homes or village shops. As soon as the summer and autumn produce of the land have been collected in so that each household has security for the year ahead, then an economic pilgrimage must be made to the plain's bazaars for the essentials of life that the Gurkhas themselves do not produce on their farms.

Throughout most of the year, a Gurkha will buy and sell in small mountain village bazaars or bazaars established by a few shop-keepers who set up their stalls on a set day each week or each month in low passes in the hills or near the confluence of several streams or the convergence of several routes. To such small bazaars, the people of several valley communities will congregate, the bazaars being so set up that each valley has the same distance to travel to market. In these bazaars, however, only very basic trading can be done and there is neither choice nor excitement nor are there luxury items such as umbrellas or shiny lamps to light the home. Hence once a year, partly for economic needs and partly as a stimulus and reward in the calm after the agricultural hiatus of the wet monsoon and attendant rice culture, the men and the boys, sometimes accompanied by women, turn their thoughts south to the plains where the major bazaars and townships lie.

Items for Trade

Salt, paraffin, woven cloth and household vessels for cooking or for storage purposes in cupboardless mountain homes are the items that must be bought or bartered for in lowland bazaars. To gain such commodities, a Gurkha will carry south whatever agricultural surplus he believes he can spare along with plaited straw sleeping mats or several thick wool blankets or winnowing trays that he has made over the months. Animals may also be taken on the hoof for sale. A mountain blacksmith will carry his khukuris to trade with and pastoralists from the higher mountain valleys will bring wool and pigs' bristles to barter with. Where an aspect favours the tobacco plant, pressed tobacco leaf is carried south to be sold and sometimes medicinal plants, herbs and roots are carried to plains doctors. Exotic items such as the musk sack of the musk ox, or

incense plants are ones that sell for high prices amongst the lowlanders who throng the bazaars.

Anatomy of a Journey

The men of a village generally make the trip together, taking some youths along to break them to the routine, toughen them and give them the experience of the trail. There are dangers on the trail if a man travels alone. Wild animals take their toll in certain isolated areas and thieves may attack the hardy traveller who travels alone if they believe he is carrying anything of value. Men thus travel in groups and each group is a well-disciplined whole that stops, starts and camps on the orders of the elder leaders. Stopping-places for each meal and each

Below: A professional Sunwar porter hired by the author to help carry kit essential for a long mountain trek. Some porters carry enormous loads, sometimes more then their own body weights, and even small children carry heavy loads of rock salt home from lowland bazaars.

Opposite: The interior of a small shop in the main lowland bazaar of Pokhara, W. Nepal. The young shopkeeper mother will have opened her shop at dawn to wait for local customers and for the people of the mountains to appear.

night's sleep are long since well established and known to all, carefully measured out by trial over the years by the length of march that a heavily laden man can be expected to travel each day.

The men and boys carry great loads that stagger the imagination. Men will carry 100 pounds for the single eight or even ten day trip to the plains and small boys often carry their own body weights in rock salt in baskets on their backs. The Gurkhas go bare-footed in the hills and the soles of their feet become pad-like with many layers of extra skin that then crack open and deeply split the soles of their feet. The very weight of the baskets causes their feet to become slightly splayed and their heads are thrust deep into their shoulders by the pull of the headbands. They see only the track immediately before them and beneath their feet and they are unable to raise their heads or eyes due to the pull of the baskets. It is only during pauses for breath that they can ease their neck muscles, look around and see the country they are passing through.

The travellers have a smell of their own, a walk of their own and a language of their own. They smell of all the things they carry and they smell of them all at once. You can smell the paraffin and the new cloth and the varied produce of the fields as the earthy traders shuffle past you, their large, wedge-shaped feet raising small scurries of dust as they plod along. The language of the trail consists of a series of grunts and gasps and low whistles that seem, as if by magic, to regulate the pace of the group, call up the slackers and tell everybody when it is time to go and when to stop. Despite his outsized load and his aching muscles, the traveller is always ready to talk with you, the headband lifted momentarily from his brow so that he can look up and see the stranger who has come to visit his land. Courteous, helpful, cheerful and kind, one never feels lonely with such wonderful companions on the trail beside you.

In the passes they rest their loads on the square stone resting platforms, built by travellers for travellers, the heavy baskets put down on the specially constructed stone ledges that keep the baskets upright and prevent them from falling while the owners relax in the shade of the twin trees, planted by design at these resting places to create

Left: A warped bamboo bridge thrown over a turbulent tributary river in E. Nepal. *Bottom left:* Early morning travellers negotiate a more permanent suspension bridge. The plank walkway is slung from heavy chain handrails. *Above:* Happy to be alive! *Right:* Two porters loaded down with a rich man's household goods. They are eastern porters and identified as such by their 'third legs' and their khukuris, the handles towards their drawing hands. *Below:* A donkey caravan carrying rice crosses the suspension bridge at Birethanti, W. Nepal. The lead donkey carries a gay red head plume. The rice will be carried north to areas where rice is not grown due to altitude and the cold.

On the trail: *Left:* A morning meal shared at a wayside stopping place. *Below:* A midday wash and scrub by two porters in the waters of an ice-cold mountain river. *Bottom-left:* The cold has won and frost covers the ground. These porters crouch under their hill blankets round a meagre fire and wait for dawn.

Left: A small Limbu boy with a resting-stick ('tekuwa'). His seat is of plaited bamboo covered in hide.
Opposite: The pleasures of the trail are the simple things in life: friendship, shared meals, resting in shade, drinking ice-cold water, climbing towards winds that blow in mountain passes and bathing in rivers when the sun is hot and the morning meal is being prepared.

A porter and his large carrying basket silhouetted against the rising sun. Near Bhojpur, E. Nepal.

Porter traffic on their way home use stepping-stones to cross a tributary stream.

Below: Brightly coloured carved prayer stones of a Buddhist shrine at Dhorpatan, central W. Nepal. The prayers are etched out in Tibetan lettering and were originally set up there by Tibetan refugees.
Below right: A wayside effigy shrine set up to appease departed spirits. Near Jumla, W. Nepal.

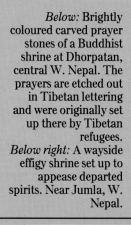

breezes, collect the dust and offer shade to weary men. One tree is a male and one is a female, the Gurkha hoping for a productive union and so more shade elsewhere some day on the hot route south.

Generosity and Kindness

The generosity of the hill peoples knows few limits. They are especially kind to travellers because they are travellers themselves and know the hardships and the discomforts of the trail. Hospitality is the right of the traveller and the Gurkha never forgets this and will never refuse it. In some places, pitchers of cold water are dug into the ground to keep them cool or are placed in the shade beside the trail for thirsty people to drink from at will. In others, the village people build and then maintain small rest houses where the traveller can find rest and shelter at nightfall. These rest houses are uninhabited and exist solely for travellers. There is never any question of payment and householders do not expect thanks for their kindness. Whatever they may do for strangers who come to their doors, they know they themselves can expect when it is their turn once more to make their way south.

A Day's March

They are on the trail well before it is light and generally move until 10 o'clock and the sun is well up before stopping for the first meal of the day. Having stopped, a well oiled routine of firewood collection and fire-making is revealed and the few fire-blackened cooking vessels and bamboo cooking-oil containers are unstrapped from the baskets. The meal will be of rice and split-lentil soup with perhaps a green vegetable. Only the black lentils take long to cook and soon the meal is ready. The flat stirring ladle then carefully gives each man an equal share of each type of food and a small bag of rock salt is passed around for communal use. Caps are doffed and a few grains of rice put aside by each man beyond his plate as an offering to the gods for the food and before beginning to eat each will wish the others a pleasant meal and then there is absolute silence as right hands clear the plates of food.

The meal is soon over, the pots scoured with ash and river silt and drying out in the sun as the travellers chat and smoke a little longer before turning once more to the trail

Above: Three porters wait for fellow travellers to reach them in the pass. It will soon be sunrise and they now have only the long downhill to the lowland market ahead of them. *Below:* An important fellow traveller — the postman, who carries mail over a set leg of a mountain route. Postmen move fast and generally alone, announcing their presence and telling all to give way by means of the cluster of small bells they carry attached to a spear they have for defence against robbers and wild animals.

and their heavy loads. The next stop of the day may be at a teahouse where tea or cool refreshing rice beer may be bought if funds permit. Then it is on until the late afternoon when the night stopping-place and sleeping-place is reached and the baskets put down for the final time that day. The evening meal is a joyous one with the day's work at an end and the firesides are merry with the happy banter of the travellers. A second rice meal inside them and the men turn to argument at one fireside while at another the melodious note of a bamboo flute or the throbbing, compelling beat of a small hill drum draws the men there into dance and song.

Before the cold night air has properly reached the camp fires, the men are asleep, very near to the fire-places for the warmth from the heated ground and hot beds of ash. As the winter night temperatures fall, so sleep in the early pre-dawn hours is fitful and hill blankets are pulled closer to chilled bodies although these are already closely huddled for group warmth. The frost wins and the sleepers rouse to move on into another day before the dawn comes. Only thus will blood flow again in cold cramped limbs, and anyway, it is as well to climb uphill in the chill of the morning before the sun gets up to add its heat to the upward toil.

The Carrying Baskets

The large baskets that the eastern men carry have narrow bases and open out towards the top. They are a flat conical shape and they carry a great deal. Packing them is a science that only a hill Gurkha adequately understands and goods are piled high well beyond the tops of the baskets and are strapped down by cords. The baskets have shoulder straps that keep the baskets on the back when the headband is removed and let fall on the chest of the wearer as he rests. It is, however, the headband that takes the full weight of the basket and the Gurkha's forehead and neck muscles do most of the straining. The arms play little part, apart from slipping in the T-shaped stick beneath the basket at halts. A small sweat-rag attached to the basket at the end of a length of cord used for steadying the load is held in the Gurkha's free hand and the baskets may be garlanded with marigold flowers as offerings to the gods of the trail for a safe journey and to the gods of plenty to fill the baskets with lowland luxuries.

A colourful wayside bazaar in E. Nepal. Heavily laden travellers rest their loads while perusing goods offered for sale. The site is shaded by trees, one male and one female and planted here to give shade and create breezes. The stone platforms in the background allow heavy baskets to be put down securely in upright positions while the owners prepare a meal or relax over a bowl of cool rice beer.

Above: A Newari shopkeeper in a lowland bazaar smokes his small hand-held 'hookah' water-pipe as he awaits custom. The base of the pipe below the smoker's hand holds the water that the smoke is drawn through and is made from a single large nut of certain trees.
Below: The serene countenance of a holy man from southern India. He was on pilgrimage to Muktinath in northern Nepal.

Top: A khukuri stall at Sakranti, E. Nepal. Here village blacksmiths bring their wares for sale. *Above:* Mountain village bazaars such as this one at Sakranti are held on set days each week and last all day. Apart from allowing people to trade, they afford opportunities for people to meet to settle business, pass on news, collect letters and plan marriages.

Above: The doughnut seller of Dailekh Bazaar, W. Nepal. *Left:* A wayside fortuneteller reading palms. *Above right:* This fellow traveller, as many mountain folk are wont to do, continued to work at his spinning both while walking and when at rest. In certain parts of W. Nepal men also knit when on the trail.
Right: While in the mountains tending flocks of sheep, men weave baskets from bamboo to take them for sale to lowland bazaars. Such baskets are used for carrying such things as chickens, hens, eggs, oranges and piglets.

Here a small boy on his very first trip to the plains is perched high on top of his father's basket; there a sick person is being carried to a lowland doctor in a specially cut down basket on a friend's back. Should it rain, then a folding shelter made out of leaves, pressed and sandwiched flat between a bamboo lattice, is opened to cover both the precious goods in the basket and also the head and shoulders of the carrier. The night blanket is slipped between the basket and the carrier's skin. In addition to his back load the Gurkha will carry his khukuri ready in his waistband, the handle towards his drawing hand. In the purse behind the khukuri will be the flint and tinder that Gurkhas still use for fire-making when on the trail.

In Lowland Bazaars

Arriving at the main bazaar, the older men earnestly bargain and haggle for top prices for their goods and the youths and boys, excited at this annual trip to the plains, tour the shops in wonder and gaze at the strange people and sights of the plains. Too soon, however, the fathers will seek them out for the return journey, the baskets loaded with necessities and even with a few luxuries for the wives and daughters who stayed behind... a new piece of cloth for a bodice, some bangles or some special silk for very special occasions. A torch is proudly shown to other men and a new umbrella tested in the sun. In the baskets may be secreted also, as surprises for friends, cigarettes, matches, bars of soap, or a new Nepali hat.

The lowland bazaars are hot, dusty places, however, and the noise is such that a man cannot properly hear himself think. The mountain men top the pass above the plains and look back and down as dawn breaks. The lowlands are still deep in shadow but to the north, the sun is already lighting up their mountains. Towards their homes they move with their heavy loads to present their small gifts to those who await them and to bring to the villages the news and gossip of the lowland bazaars. The baskets unloaded in their homes and the economic pilgrimage is over for another year. The air is pure again and dust-free and the water, cold and sweet.

THROUGH THE AGES

Let it Be a Son

EVERY GURKHA FATHER hopes his first born may be a son for sons can share with the father the heavy work on the land and can run the homestead and plough the paddy fields in the father's old age. Only a son can leave the homestead and earn an income that will enhance the way of life of the entire family group by providing money to buy more land, build a better house or educate younger brothers and sisters. Only a son can follow a father into a Gurkha Regiment to seek his fortune there and travel the world outside the mountain valley that he was born into. It is in the mountain villages that the Gurkhas, as boys, are forged as men.

Growing Up

A boy child has to be hardy to survive and grow up strong in the mountains for life is hard and soon eliminates the weaklings. Through the ages the young boy will be fashioned and conditioned by a way of life that gives him confidence in himself and a sturdy independence that is refreshing to behold. He will live most of his early days, once weaned, out in the open air playing or hunting or watching his father working in the fields. His home will be a single unit, one-roomed house and he will play inside by the fire-pit set into the foot-smoothed, dung-smeared earthen floor. At night, when tiredness overcomes the young, there is no undressing: a thick hill blanket is wrapped around them and they sleep on low sleeping platforms or on the floor near to the fire-pit.

There are few initiation ceremonies to boyhood beyond the priest's blessings when the boy is named and when the boy is given his first meal of rice and his first haircut. A small shirt will cover his upper body when he is young but his lower limbs will be naked for ease of hygiene until, at about 3 or 4 years, he adopts a small loin-cloth and then sometime later, male nether garments. While still a child his ears will be pierced by metal pins or thorns to take earrings and the pierced holes kept open by means of small wooden plugs until the wounds heal around them. The boys, depending on family inclination and tribal habit, may then wear earrings until their late teens or even until early manhood.

A boy will seldom hear his name used or called. Instead he will be referred to as the 'first-born' or 'second-born'. This is because if a name were used or shouted over the hillsides by a mother calling to her son, evil spirits or a witch might get to hear the name and thereby have the boy within their power and be able to do the boy harm by having captured his name. A captured name may lead to a captured soul.

From early days the boys are integrated into the routine of the homestead and are given work to do. They fetch and carry water and fodder and small boys can be seen high up in the trees cutting the succulent foliage for the herds of goats. They often spend most of the day away from the home carefree and happy with their own company or that of one or two other children. They become accustomed to being cold and wet and

Left: Two young boys of the priestly caste, close friends, share a hill wrap together against the morning chill at Takum, W. Nepal. *Opposite:* Gurung mother with yellow beads, Thulsar, W. Nepal.

Above left: Collecting the morning water. *Above:* Greetings from a small girl from the porch of her home. *Left:* Poorly clad against the cold, this little boy was busy carrying animal manure to spread over and help fertilize his father's fields. *Right:* The headman's daughter: a pretty Magar girl, her earrings temporarily replaced by small wooden plugs, in the sun beside her home, Lukum, W. Nepal.

hungry and happy cries and shouts can be heard from the mountain sides as the boys cover the family grazing grounds with the herds. They develop and never lose, acute senses of hearing, sight and sound. A Gurkha boy is used to looking across his deep valley from one side to the other and searching the far slopes for the movement of people and of flocks. Their eyes detect movement very quickly and their wonderful senses of hearing and of smell are totally unblunted when eventually they join the regiments.

The Learning Process

Some time later in life at about 9 or 10 years they are to be found during the dry months of the year in the upland cattle pens alone with the animals. There, they live with a supply of flour for themselves and salt for the animals, while the latter graze the good grasses and produce their young. The animals are milked and the warm milk drunk by the herd boys. The youngsters soon learn the ways of the animals and of what life is all about: about creation and about death when a weakling calf is born into a mountain environment. They talk to the animals and give them all a name, each based on some physical peculiarity or peculiarity of colour.

They soon learn the names and the uses of the trees and the plants they are surrounded by. A boy will know what tree to cut to provide the hardest, pest-resistant beams for his home and its roof. They know what woods are best to cut for making ploughs and khukuri handles and which trees the ferrymen seek to burn out their ferries from. The boys learn early the fact that there are many different types of bamboo in the hills and that bamboo has a thousand uses on the farms. Here are bamboo walls and bamboo roofs; there a woman carries and stores the stream water in sections of bamboo. Here a farmer has brought drinking and irrigation water to his home by leading it down a hillside in bamboo pipes; there a small school boy is writing upon bamboo paper while his brother plays on a bamboo flute.

The boys become very practical with their hands and handle khukuris and agricultural implements naturally and skillfully. They shape and make for themselves the things that more developed communities are forced to go to shops and

Above: 'Isn't life fun?' Two happy little friends of Kasur village, W. Nepal.
Right: The old man of Jubing, E. Nepal.

spend money on. A Gurkha boy cutting down a tree will chop with even stroke, minimum effort and by putting the khukuri blade in exactly the same cut each time. They know what vines to cut and twist together as lashings and they are expert at cutting and bundling grass and straw into sheaves. They know how to make rope and string and they are skilled at tying knots and at making split bamboo into baskets and fences. They plait their own headbands and make the short tough halters and ropes that tether the animals out to wooden stakes in the ground. A boy knows where to look for and find the colourful red and white clays that decorate and colour the external walls of his home, and what clays are best to use to mould the hard clay pellets that Gurkha boys then shoot from bows to kill birds and small animals.

Frugality

Nothing is so useless that it is thrown away. Every tree, every shrub, every stone and every piece of wood has a thousand uses. If a grain of rice is dropped into a stream while the rice is being washed, the offending grain is carefully and solemnly searched for and put back into the washing bowl before the meal is progressed with. Empty bottles are worth their weight in gold for carrying paraffin up from the lowlands and for storing it in the home. Any old box or tin is highly prized as a medium of storage in the cupboardless homes of the hills. Likewise, although there is only a little actual money circulation and money transaction in Nepal, everybody, even the little goatherd boys out on the hillsides, knows the value of money and of gold.

Towards Maturity

The boys, as they advance in years, learn a lot from their fathers. Fathers take their sons in hand early in life and teach them the secrets of life and of how the farm and home must be run. They soon wean the boys away from women-work and child-work and teach them their roles as males in the household. A father teaches his son how to yoke the family bullocks to the plough and how to wrestle the plough through wet paddy and dry maize fields. The boys must learn how to control and turn the animals while keeping the plough upright, and, by putting their own weight on the plough, to force the metal point to bite deeply and so turn a better furrow in the soil.

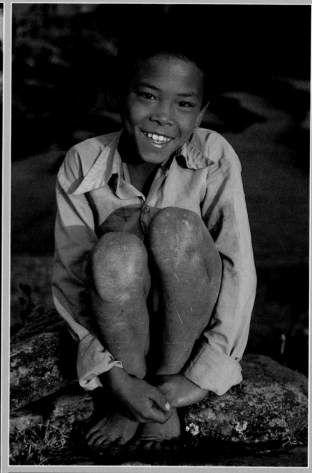

Left: Magar boy with large earrings in the sunlit porch of his home in W. Nepal. *Above:* A winsome smile from a small Gurung boy in a blue shirt, Tulsar, W. Nepal. *Below left:* Daughter of the family priest: a courteous salutation from a young fellow traveller. *Below:* The Limbu matriarch of Mele, E. Nepal. All her sons have served as soldiers.

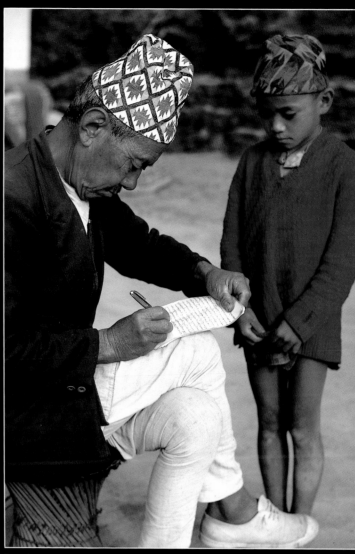

Above: A father, an ex-officer himself, writes to a serving son. A would-be soldier looks on.

Above: Wrapped in his hill blanket, this small Magar boy of W. Nepal was on his way to school when he met the author. Bare-footed and bare-limbed, he is tough and enduring.
Right: A male of the Ale clan plaits a rope halter for his animals. Men and women are all expert plaiters of bamboo and rope.

Opposite: Gurung patriarch of Dadra Gaun, W. Nepal. About to leave home on a journey, he has been blessed and given flowers for a safe passage. He has also been given a 'tika', the vermilion mark on his forehead that signifies he has worshipped and been blessed by an elder.

An elderly Gurung decked out in all her finery and wearing all the traditional jewellery befitting a woman of her age and status. She was the wife of a Gurkha officer who had been decorated several times for bravery.

As well as living a life near to nature that gives him endurance and a healthy body with senses, razor sharp, the Gurkha boy also finds time for a basic schooling and has always had to consider his social contract with life by considering marriage. Even today a boy may have his future bride marked out for him from early on in his life by his parents but more commonly boys now marry later in life and select their own brides free from complete parental dominance although parents may still have a large say in the eventual match.

The Urge to Leave Home

When there are several sons in a family and the older ones have reached their teens, the father may well consider sending one of them off to earn a living in the army, thereby ensuring an income to the home and easing the pressure of too many sons on the household, not yet able to move away with their wives to set up their own homes elsewhere. The family may well be too poor to allow the latter and the father be unwilling to subdivide his small acreage amongst his sons for yet a few more years to come. A life for one or two sons in the army does, therefore, mean considerable economic relief for a family and the enhanced opportunities that a son's wages will bring are most eagerly sought after.

The youths of the village, having spent their boyhoods in the relative seclusion of the mountain valleys, are eager, of course, to go off and join the army and see what lies beyond the plains, the limits of their travels so far. Few ever travel east or west of their own deep valleys or ever visit Kathmandu. Their only outlet is a southward leading trail to the plains by means of the economic pilgrimage to lowland bazaars there once a year.

There is Something About a Soldier . . .

Boys will have seen soldiers, however, home on leave and pension on the mountain trails and will have talked to soldiers in their own villages or at the homes of friends. There is something about a soldier, home on leave, the bringer of supplies, luxuries, radios, pressure lamps and news of far flung places. How modern and smart their clothes are and what fascinating things they have done and have to say! Not content with life on the farm and envying others who have already joined the army and gone off to seek excitement,

Boys must learn how to repair paddy walls and about rice culture and how to control the irrigation waters on the paddy terraces. They must be able to hunt properly and to help the animals in times of difficult delivery of their young and know how to take black leeches from the nostrils of the buffaloes. They must also learn the market value of animals and produce and be able to do business in a bazaar and for the purchase and sale of land. In the quiet of the evenings or when resting in the sun, a father will also softly tell his sons about religion, of the good and evil spirits that inhabit their mountain world, of family secrets and about his own plans for the future and continuance of the family group as a whole.

At the end of the cycle of life: A funeral pyre *(top)* of an elderly Chhetri of W. Nepal. The body lies under its safron-coloured shroud while the man's son and helpers prepare the pyre. Not all tribes burn their dead on river banks: some bury their dead in special burial grounds on hilltops high above tribal villages. *Left:* The pyre is now alight, fat having been smeared on the wood to ensure a swift consummation. *Above:* Another cremation, this time on the Mewa Khola, E. Nepal. The pyre was that of a Limbu woman and male relatives with bamboo poles turn the body and stir the fire to ensure rapid and complete incineration.

Above: Two brothers on their way to school pause in the sunlit porch of a wayside rest house, built and maintained solely for travellers. One has his school slate with him. *Below:* Young Limbu boy with a 'karda' — the skinning knife that is always carried in the sheath of every mountain khukuri and which has a thousand uses in the hands of a yeoman hill farmer. *Opposite:* The children ensure that life goes on. Here a small Gurung girl of Bejang, W. Nepal poses in the pass above her home.

youths do become restless and watch the mountain paths eagerly for the visiting recruiter who could take them to the plains for examination, and if successful, for enlistment. Only if the youths go with such an established recruiter do they stand a good chance of entering the military; a youth going on his own would not get consideration until these established recruiters had presented their full quotas of youths for examination.

When the father will not willingly let a boy go with the recruiter, many leave their homesteads secretly by simply slipping away without telling anyone and then making their way to join a recruiter or directly to the plains in the hope that somehow they will become enlisted. Boys who fail to get places in the army generally seek other employment in the townships on the plains, or may even travel towards India for work rather than return home either because they fear the anger of parents they had left secretly and without permission, or because the loss of face is just too great to bear when they were sent with their father's blessings to join his former regiment but have been turned down.

Whether they are sent with their parents' consent, however, with garlands round their necks as blessings for success and a safe journey, or whether they have slipped away, penniless and with but a pocketful of food to seek their fortunes, the youths are now mature and the equal of the world they seek to enter. They are sturdy and developing fast towards their physical prime. They are skilled with their hands and can see and hear and smell things that other civilisations have lost the ability to perceive any more. They are physically and mentally resilient and they are obedient, proud and bold.

Honest and eager to become soldiers they look the recruiter in the eye and answer his questions with confidence knowing that there are none present better than they themselves. Successful, they become soldiers and serve on contracts around the world for an average of 15 years, returning home once in 3 years on leave to see their parents, families, brothers and sisters. Wherever they go, they take with them the priceless characteristics they have developed through the ages and which make these herd boys of Nepal the cheerful warriors of Gurkha Regiments throughout the world.

INTO THE REGIMENTS

Red Coats and Gurkha Warriors

BORN OUT OF NINETEENTH CENTURY FRICTION between British India and Nepal, the Brigade of Gurkhas is founded and based on the respect and admiration of one nation for another. The Red Coats of the East India Company saw in the enduring and tenacious Gurkha qualities that they greatly admired and respected. Here was a worthy foe; doughty in battle, brave and fiercely loyal to the cause, dignified and proud when at peace. What allies such men would make! And, in these strange British soldiers with whom war had brought them into contact and who (after they themselves) were bonny fighters, the Gurkhas felt they had found something by way of a bond, of fellow feeling, of kinship — call it what you will — with fellow warriors that attracted them into service with the armies of British India. The Gurkha felt at home with his erstwhile foe and felt that he would be looked after by the likes of the military in the regiments of India.

There was thus genuine affection by the tall Red Coat for the diminutive Gurkha who never seemed to stop smiling, was always polite and who always wanted to be friendly. Fascinated, the English soldiers watched the cheerful mountaineers as they drove themselves to perfection, trained endlessly and earnestly until all faults were eradicated and who were dedicated towards becoming professional infantrymen, second to none. The bond between the Gurkha and his English counterpart is an indefinable thing based on respect for the other's qualities, characteristics, background and way of life.

And so today, based on over 170 years of history and tested in bloody wars down the decades, there is this mystic bond between a contract hill Gurkha from a central Asian kingdom and the British. Honed to perfection by their dedicated training and borne into battle on rigid standards of loyalty and discipline, the Gurkhas have been allies of Great Britain in all her major conflicts these last 170 years. Thousands have died outside their mountain homes on foreign battlefields for reasons and causes they never questioned.

Their ability as soldiers, loyalty as allies and qualities as men, are enduring and have stood the test of time.

The Search for Sound Bodies

During the dry season each year when the rice crop has been harvested, the recruiters return to the recruiting depots with their batches of recruits. The recruiters have been out in the hills and in the mountain valleys for about two months seeking youths who are ready to leave home with their father's blessing to enter military service. And so at the turn of each year the recruiting depots are crowded with youths all seeking to enter one of the Gurkha Regiments. All are eager and earnestly plead their cases for a chance to go before the recruiting officers. Stripped of their mountain clothes, they fall in in serried ranks, their brown, dusky bodies naked but for shorts or loin-cloths, so that bodies and limbs are seen to the best advantage.

Above: Three would-be soldiers, these Magar boys of Lukum in W. Nepal will scan the mountain paths eagerly for signs of the 'gallawala' — the 'recruiter'. He is their key to a life in a regiment away from Nepal and across the "black water", far from home. *Opposite:* The finished article. A proud Gurkha in service in Singapore.

Left: 'We want to be soldiers too!' These two small Rai boys have relatives serving in both Indian and British Gurkha Regiments.

Below left: '. . . and so do we!' The three sons of a retired Gurkha Captain on the veranda of their homestead in W. Nepal.

Below: The recruiting cycle beings when the recruiters arrive at the recruiting depots with their batches of hill boys for selection. Here a group, or 'galla', of eastern boys waits to enter the depot. The recruiter is on the left. He himself is an ex-serviceman and is paid a wage as well as so much for each boy successfully recruited.

Right: Stripped of mountain clothes to show bodies off to the best advantage. The letters and numbers on each boy's chest were to help categorize and keep track of each potenital recruit amongst the many hundreds who flooded into the depots.

The recruiting officers make the preliminary survey of the youths and sort them out into categories based on their bodily characteristics of height and weight. Here an especially small youth stands on tiptoe to add an inch to his diminutive height, there another wills the scales to put pounds on him and may even have stones secreted about his person in order to tip the scales in his favour. All heave their chests up with great gulps of air and mightily held breaths while chest measurements are being made. A member of the recruiting staff marks their chests with strange symbols in coloured ink to indicate one knows not what.

Then it is off to see a man called "Doctor Sahib", an extraordinary specimen in a white coat who prods your body, looks in your mouth and listens to your chest with long tubes stuck in his ears. Such extraordinary behaviour. One is stood in front of a machine that takes a photograph of your chest, and all without hurting! While waiting to see "Doctor Sahib" long hill locks are cut by an uncompromising barber who offers no choice of style. And so for two days it goes on, this search for sound limbs and healthy constitutions.

On a set day, once all the medical tests are over, the youths are once again in serried ranks for the results of the examinations to be made known. For those who have passed, there is a feeling of elation that so much has been accomplished; for those who have been rejected there is the heartbreak of the stigma of failure. Few will return home to disappointed parents and friends who might jibe... the disappointed ones will drift to seek work and consolation elsewhere, perhaps returning home at a much later date when the wound has healed and certainly not until they have attempted to join the army again in another year's time.

While the recruiting goes on, the youths who have come down to the depots have to be fed. Huge mounds of rice are prepared along with mountains of vegetables, curries and split-lentil soup. The youths have never seen so much food in such a small space on earth before and large platefuls of rice follow large platefuls of rice into hungry bellies.

For those who have met the physical and medical standards, even more exciting days lie ahead. Clerks will ask you all manner of

The recruiting process goes on:
Right: Chest measurements: a mightily held breath by a would-be recruit. *Right below:* Not daring to look down, but willing the scales to add pounds to his weight! *Above and below:* A struggle with buttons at the Quartermaster's Store. (Buttons are still not common in mountain villages where tunics, bodices etc all have ties to keep them closed and in place.) *Opposite (top):* Successful candidates take the oath under the supervision and eagle eye of a retired officer now employed on recruiting duties, and *(below)* the strangeness of that the very first salute.

Author's Note: These photographs were taken in 1961 and the intervening years have seen changes. Fewer recruits now wear loin-cloths, some uniform styles have altered and some recruiting procedures have been modified.

The determination of the hill boys makes them tough fighters. Their nature is to grit their teeth and hang on and their superb eyesight as trained hunters makes them marksmen with most weapons.

Opposite (top left): Trainers of recruits are dedicated men who watch over their charges with zeal, seek perfection and put them through their paces with great enthusiasm. *(Right):* The bugles, pipes and drums of one Gurkha unit, led by the Drum-major in his magnificent sash.

Above: On public duty in the United Kingdom: Red Coat and diminutive Gurkha.
Opposite: The turnout, bearing, weapons and khukuris of all Gurkhas are thoroughly inspected each day before they leave for their operational posts.

questions and in strange dialects about what your age is, who your mother was, your wife's name and where you were born. Some youths sign attestation papers, others solemnly place an inked thumb in the generous space provided for signatures. All are a bit puzzled by the rigmarole and complexity of these signing on procedures.

After the perplexing days of the "Doctor Sahib" and the clerks with their endless questions comes the exciting trip to the stores where the recruits are given an initial basic scale of clothing that will serve them until they reach the training depots. What an exciting time! Each gets a kit bag full of knobbly things that cascade out to reveal themselves as things called shirts, trousers, socks and sandals. Mountain clothes are taken off again and either handed over to be burnt or to a fellow traveller who will see them safely back to mountain homes. Then comes the excitement and pleasure of pulling on for the very first time a pair of trousers that button down the front; of putting on a shirt that has buttons on the cuffs and all down the chest and of the thrill of stockings and leather sandals that buckle on the feet. On the head goes the warm woollen cap comforter and the transformation is complete — the mountain herd boy is no more; behold the young Gurkha soldier.

Final Days in Nepal

Kitted out, the recruits take the oath of allegiance and then await the aircraft that will take them across the "black water" of the oceans, away from their mountain homes and Nepal, to places their fathers have talked about but where these places are only the gods know at this stage. While they await their onward move, their bodies are given physical work that develops their sense of balance and rhythm and they are introduced to the mysteries of simple drill and physical training. Their feet are still hard from the trails of their youth and cannot yet be encased in boots. The hard skin of the soles of their feet is thus allowed to soften and become supple in sandals, worn initially for only a few hours each day.

Across the "Black Water"

A great roaring noise, worse than a thousand hill avalanches, and the machine

They are taught to move with their weapons both with speed, closing resolutely with an adversary, and also silently, using all their pent-up skills learned as stalkers of game as young boys in their mountain homes.

takes off to muttered Hindu prayers. How small the houses and villages look from up here! Is that really a river down there and is that my home? How will this machine ever climb the mountains ahead and how can it navigate with no village elder on board? Soon it is night outside and bodies, drained of adrenalin and exhausted by excitement, sleep, as the throb of engines forces eyes to shut and heads to droop forward.

It is at the training depots that these recruits are taken in hand by competent, dedicated Gurkha officers and non-commissioned officers and turned into soldiers. They are brought to a peak of perfection over a period of 10 months hard, demanding training during which they are taught how to handle themselves and their weapons in battle. Jealously watched over by zealous instructors, the young recruits are honed to perfection and given confidence in themselves and in their arms. At the end of ten months, on a large parade, the newly fledged soldiers will march past their General with an élan and a panache that only Gurkhas possess. And so to the regiments, the sons follow the fathers for full careers that will take them to many strange lands.

Johnny Gurkha

Wherever they are called to serve or whatever they will be asked to do, they will do with a dedication, zeal, enthusiasm and loyalty that is stimulating to behold. Never complaining, trusting implicitly in their officers and NCOs, they go about their tasks, now sweating in the heat and gloom of jungle swamps, now shivering in the rain and biting wind of other lands where the rocks permit no lee. Even in the most appalling conditions they will hang on and endure until relief arrives. Gentlemen fighters, they bear no grudges and are sympathetic towards the vanquished. Their razor-sharp senses, self-discipline and hunting instincts are assets that make them doughty foes. Small-limbed and light on their feet they are capable of moving forward silently like shadows until they are close to their foe. Then, at close quarters, they wield their khukuris with deadly effect.

Wherever they serve, they will make friends and will be respected for their

smartness and efficiency and will be loved because they smile and are such happy warriors. The regimental name and their Gurkha oath are everything and even in pain they do not cry out. Many serve and bear arms for over 30 years and become illustrious figures in their own rights, the very pillars of their regiments. Power never goes to their heads, however, and they always remember their own humble beginnings — of the struggle to be recruited and to join the regiment as young hill boys those many long years ago.

And, when it is all over, and with honour they claim their pensions and leave the regiments, then it is to return whence they came, to the steep-sided valleys and mountain sides of their homeland. Here they pick up again the threads of their lives as farmers interrupted several decades ago. And in the dry season now there is time, they will sit by the sun-heated walls of their homesteads and tell young boys of the village of their lives in the regiments, of battles won, of friends and friendship and of life in lands across the "black water". And as they talk they kindle fires in the breasts of the young who listen to them so that they too, when the time is ripe, will slip away to seek as their elders did, fame and a place in the Gurkha Regiments.

Top: An old 'Subedar' ('Captain') of Dadra Gaon in traditional Nepali hat, eyes still keen, uses an old pair of binoculars (a relic of his wars) to seek out movement far on distant slopes. *Above:* With a scarf round his neck and one round his head against the morning chill, a veteran of many campaigns and the holder of two Military Crosses for bravery sits by the ochre wall of a homestead. Red poinsettia have been put behind his ear and on his head as a sign of welcome and respect.

THE GURKHA AS A SOLDIER

The Contract Soldier

A S CONTRACT SOLDIERS, with a record of loyalty and single-minded devotion to their officers, the Gurkhas are unique. Stubbornly loyal to those whom they recognise, their endurance and bravery are legend. Set on terraced mountain slopes where time moves slowly, the homesteads of Nepal send their young men to serve in an outside world that is galloping ahead in a frantic rush to reach the stars and unlock the secrets of creation. It is remarkable that the unimaginative and phlegmatic mountain Gurkha does not succumb to future shock as he steps off the aircraft to be inducted into the àrmy amid the teeming rush of humanity and the sophistication of foreign parts. But he does not succumb; he may blink and look with awe for a fleeting second or two, but generally his expression does not change and he very quickly accepts his new surroundings, not by aping what he sees but by maintaining his own values and standards and traditions within the military cantonments he joins.

There may be some slight envy at the apparent ease of life he sees before him but there is no great desire to become part of it: the Gurkha seeks employment to able to save and send back money to his own country, there to raise the quality of life for his family left behind to the harsh life of subsistence farming that he has broken free from by entering the military. Every Gurkha's period of service is conditioned throughout by the knowledge that one day it will end and that he will then have to return whence he came. Throughout his service, therefore, and in whatever rank, he will lead a simple, modest life, putting aside all the money he can to invest in his mountain home.

Service is for Life

A Gurkha Regiment is a very close-knit community with continuity of service an outstanding feature of its way of life. The Gurkha comes to serve for life or until the rules for pension debar him from further service. A man can thus expect to have security of service for a minimum of 15 years, at which time he must leave on pension unless he is going to merit promotion to higher rank. Beyond the 15 years men serve on until they reach their rank ceiling with the better men becoming Gurkha Officers and serving until they have some 30 years unbroken service behind them.

Sons follow fathers and young brothers, elder brothers, so that whole villages and valleys become firmly wedded to the Gurkha Regiments and there is an ages-long contact and continued interchange of men between the regiments and the Gurkhas' homes in the Himalayas. Continuity of service in the Gurkha Regiments, allied to the close blood relationships that exist amongst the serving men, give the regiments great cohesion and strength. The men serve best amongst close relations and are loathe to step out of line or let their comrades down when word can so

Opposite: Contract hill Gurkhas on parade in Singapore. *Left:* With the Guards in London.

easily be carried home and passed around. The feeling that they have not succeeded or that they may have let their regiment down is not one that a Gurkha wants to live with.

An officer on trek in Nepal can visit his own soldiers who may be on pension or on leave, when he visits their villages. Meeting old soldiers is a humbling experience. Their faces light up as they recognise you and there is a warm handshake as they take your hand in both of theirs and hold it as memories flood back. They greatly welcome visits from their officers and the chance to sit down and, having offered hospitality, then to recount tales and relive battles won those many years ago. You can tell the old soldiers by their bearing and the way they stiffen as you introduce yourself.

Seniority and Promotion

Seniority is understood and almost revered by the Gurkhas so that the senior man is expected to speak up and be the spokesman for those junior to him in years or service. When it comes to promotions, however, difficulties and misunderstandings can arise. The men are all the equals of each other back in their mountain homes where all men tackle the same environment and overcome it by the strength of their bodies and their strong right arms. The idea, therefore, that any one man is better than another is sometimes difficult for a Gurkha to accept and many expect that promotion can only be done by strict seniority, not by merit. All Gurkhas, therefore, aspire towards promotion and expect to get on, finding it difficult to accept when someone junior merits promotion ahead of they themselves. Such is the Gurkha's belief in his own abilities and as a man without peer amongst his own age group, that at times, a man passed over cannot reconcile the fact within himself and may ask to leave the regiment. Having said that, rank and age are everything and the senior man holding rank is the man who is listened to. Orders are pushed down the ranks scrupulously and there is no question of a man doing anything except within the strict chain of command.

The long careers that Gurkha soldiers serve means that there is great experience, professionalism and ability built into each regiment. Commanders are not continually

being faced with large turnovers of personnel nor having too many trained and experienced men leaving the regiments at the same time. Commanders are thus able to devote their time to building on training already done and on experience already gained. It is rare, except through death, for gaps to appear in the ranks due to men opting out and a man can serve for his entire service in the same platoon or sub-unit, with his commanders seldom changing and never suddenly. Men so closely bonded together know each other's strengths and weaknesses and serve admirably as a unit, men leaning on men whom they know and trust implicitly, each part of a well-oiled team and the team strong and able to withstand great shock and stress and not disintegrating even when under the very severest mental and physical pressure.

In the Company of Others

When off-duty, the Gurkha is not gregarious and he is slightly reserved when outside the confines of his cantonment or camp. Their need to save and send money home is so great, that there is little wealth left over to spend on luxuries or amusements or

Above and left: Khukuri drill: the khukuris are drawn and inspected for the keeness of their cutting edges and they must be razor sharp. It is a myth that a Gurkha, having once drawn his blade, must use it to draw blood before returning it to its scabbard again.

Left: Gurkhas are not naturally good swimmers unless born near a river in Nepal, yet as soldiers they have to be able to take themselves and their weapons and equipment across rivers and water obstacles. They are therefore taught to swim as recruits and to be confident and proficient when in water.

Above: An intent young Gurkha listens to a war story from an old soldier. *Right:* With the Chelsea Pensioners in London.

on becoming integrated with an overseas community even if the Gurkha had a desire to become so integrated. They are happiest and most relaxed with their own company, within their own kin groups or on their own. A walk round the nearest shopping centre on a Sunday afternoon when one or two members of the group may have planned to buy a shirt or a pair of shoes, or a visit in a group to a zoo or local scenic place on a picnic, easily satisfies a Gurkha and he expects and demands little more from his leisure time. Indeed, the vast majority of a Gurkha's leisure time will be spent playing games and a Gurkha is really either training or keeping himself fit on a sportsfield somewhere. A man physically involved all day in training and sports does not miss his wife so much as a man with time on his hands.

In the company of strangers, especially from other lands, the Gurkha is quiet, correct, reserved, polite, respectful, somewhat shy, and always eager to please and be friendly. He has an inborn pride and dignity that gains him automatic respect from all who have dealings with him. There is never anything servile about a Gurkha and those who insult him or treat him wrongly light a fuse of slow burning anger and resentment that may seldom manifest itself even when burning bright within the man. They are also very discerning people and very quickly sum up those they serve as people who have their interests at heart or not. Their loyalty is not blind but is a discerning loyalty. They obey the given order because the order is everything — but that does not mean that they deeply respect the person who gives it. As soldiers, they like to be ordered and organised and given crystal clear instructions. They will obey and always do exactly what they are told to do: they will not waver from the given order nor make any exceptions to it unless specifically told to.

Training

They are fastidious about keeping themselves, their bodies and clothes, and their cantonments and surroundings scrupulously clean. There is always a great scrubbing and scouring of teeth (which is important in that they are strong and are prime weapons for opening knots, taking off

'KHUKURI' or 'kukri' refers to the large curved knife that the Gurkha always carries with him in uniform and in battle. In the hands of a Gurkha, it is a formidable weapon and cutting tool. It is razor-sharp and is symbolic of him as a fighting man. The knife is essentially an agricultural implement of eastern Nepal that has been adopted for use as a fighting weapon over the centuries. As a yeoman farmer, the Gurkha uses his khukuri for a multitude of domestic and cultural tasks and the knife is always carried in the cloth waistband that a yeoman farmer wears round his waist when at work or when travelling.

The khukuri is carried in a wooden sheath (often leather-covered) and in the sheath behind the khukuri itself are carried two smaller knives: the 'chakmak', that is, a small blunt knife-shaped implement used in making fire, and the other, the 'karda', a very sharp knife used for a variety of purposes from the skinning of animals to the splitting of bamboo into long strips prior to plaiting them into baskets or mats.

Behind the 'chakmak' and the 'karda' is a small leather purse used to carry the other essentials of fire-making, namely a quartz stone and some very fine dry tinder with the substance of cotton-wool called 'jhulo', made from the bark, wood or seeds of special trees. The quartz stone is struck against the 'chakmak' and any sparks caught up in the 'jhulo' are blown upon to create fire. In a very ornate khukuri, other small implements such as a small pair of tweezers, a small spike etc are also carried.

On the cutting edge of every khukuri blade, just above the handle, is a knotch. This knotch is a Hindu fertility symbol.

They are masters of the jungle environment and completely at home in it. It holds no terrors for them and, armed with khukuris and other weapons they can spend long periods in it, alone and without relief.

bottle tops or for stripping wire) and trousers and even suits do not escape the frequent beatings with soap and water meted out to underclothes and sportswear. An officer leaves his suede shoes near soap and water at his own risk and a Gurkha Orderly automatically sweeps up all his officer's belongings in the great drive for good hygiene and clean surroundings. Trees in a cantonment are soundly shaken to make them give up their dead leaves and jungle training camps are swept bare of all deadfall so that no mosquito, snake or bug survives the onslaught on their habitat.

They train during peace with a zeal and passion that is breath-taking to behold. Slower to learn than people with more formal schooling and more advanced backgrounds than they themselves, they do take longer to train. During their recruit training days they are honed to perfection by zealous and dedicated instructors. Once in their regiments, the desire for perfection goes on and due to their natures and upbringing, repetition and repeated commands never bore them. Gurkhas, training, are quite uninhibited and are totally devoted to the task in hand. They are not shy or reticent at volunteering to try something new and there is nothing to feel embarrassed about if called upon to give a demonstration or play the part of the enemy.

There is great competition to be sent on courses and the endeavours of Gurkha soldiers burning the midnight oil to ensure success on their courses, are legend. The Gurkhas make up much ground by sheer application and dedication on courses and, once learned, lessons are meticulously followed and no detail ever forgotten. As people, they are, however, not imaginative nor able always to take the unexpected in their stride: their early life was perhaps too hard, too pressing, primitive, stark and demanding to let the mind wander far or for fertile imaginations to develop.

Apart from Sherpas (who revel in the healthy glow brought on by the snows and deep frosts of their northern winter) Gurkhas tend to dislike the cold and to dislike it intensely. In their villages, from the verandas of their homes, most see the snows but few Gurkhas actually live above the snow or frost lines. Many may see their summer

grazing lands under a heavy fall of snow for several weeks or more and the winds, if from the snow-clad Himalayas and prolonged, are ice-cold. The majority of Gurkhas, however, live in a benign climatic range and on favourable aspects where the hours of sunlight are long and hot. Only between sunset and sunrise are hill wraps needed and drawn tightly round chilled bodies. Thus when training or at war, a Gurkha is happiest when in a warm climate and is at his most miserable when enduring a combination of cold, wet conditions.

A Most Natural Fighting Man

The Gurkhas are one of the world's most natural of fighting men. To the military and to their regiments, they bring the physical and mental characteristics bred into them as mountaineers and as subsistence hill farmers from an underdeveloped land. They bring wonderful senses of sight, smell and hearing that we, in our civilization, have long since lost. Their senses are still keen and razor sharp, quite unblunted by life in a sophisticated environment. A Gurkha uses his eyes to seek out the movement of animals on distant slopes and his ears and nose are finely attuned to the sounds and smells of his habitat.

Gurkhas also have an almost uncanny sense of direction, developed out of following paths and scant trails across far-flung mountain landscapes, through miles of silent forests and up across thousands of feet of terraced mountain sides, the almost non-existent track ever changing direction and winding over streams, rocks and round paddy terrace walls. They know, by practical experience, where routes should run across any given piece of land and have a finely developed eye for terrain. Their memories for routes are also phenomenal. Their eyes automatically pick up the salient points of a track and a Gurkha, taken once over a route,

will easily find his way back and be able to retrace the complete route at a later date with ease. Whether in a city or in the gloom of a trackless jungle, they know where they are and even a series of complex right and left turns does not throw them off direction. This ability to follow the grain of the landscape, know where man-made tracks will be found and to be able to memorize a route even through trackless jungle, greatly benefits the Gurkha when he goes against an unseen enemy.

To soldiering, the Gurkha brings an excellent physique. With their powerful legs and loins, they can carry great loads over long distances and are without peer in hilly and mountainous terrain akin to their boyhood environment. Their small, neat, compact bodies are also great assets in the jungle and a Gurkha is able to move through the jungle almost ghost-like, without disturbing the jungle foliage and without sound. As natural hunters, they move forward silently, their bodies balanced and their feet, equipment and weapons making no sound.

A Gurkha patrol is an utterly silent thing, communicating by means of fleeting hand signals and the facial expressions of those in command. For the duration of a ten to fourteen day jungle patrol, the members will not speak a word to each other and only muted, whispered words may pass between commanders. Gurkhas do not fight the jungle; they are at one with it, able to hunt its animals, knowing how to use its food to

survive and always emerging fro[m] after many weeks within, with t[he] clean, their equipment intact a[nd] clothes still whole upon their b[odies]

The Order is Everything

Bold, hardy, tough, endurin[g] unimaginative, Gurkhas never [worry] about the ethics of any war or co[nflict they] get caught up in. The given orde[r] upon which they will stand until [they are] overwhelmed. Death and the thr[eat] are used to by their very upbring[ing] they do not hold back at the pro[spect of] death or of danger that may prec[ede it.] Discomfort, they are inured to fr[om] childhood and so at war the pro[spect of being] out in, and at the mercy of, the e[lements does] not in any way inhibit them. The[y are used] to nature and its extremes, unde[rstand them] and can cope with them.

They are patient, tolerant an[d calm in] the face of hold-ups, snags, delay[s and] disappointments and, in the end[, of] wounds and death. They sweep [upon the] enemy, carried forward by their [sheer] obedience and because they are s[upported] by comrades and commanders t[hey love. They] are close-bonded both by blood a[nd] mutual respect.

Even terribly wounded they [and] their tough bodies and harsh upb[ringing] enable them to endure. The job [and] the name of the regiment are eve[rything as] their direct forefathers before the[m, with] the loyalty and perseverance of t[hem]

uninterrupted and unswerving and their own
interests never encroach upon the oath of
fealty that they give.

In Battle and in Victory

Once roused and with the enemy before
them, they are deadly adversaries and
manoeuvre and skirmish with utter
professionalism. Stout-hearted, their black
hair spiky with sweat, they move forward,
lithe bodies using the ground with the skills
of the hunter. Their faces tensed and with all
their senses taut and straining, they seek out
their adversary. The firefight won, then, with
deadly effect, they close with their mountain
khukuris in their hands.

In victory, they are compassionate and
the beaten foe is never humiliated nor
mistreated. Gentle Gurkha hands tend those
in pain and a Gurkha's habit is to forgive and
forget. Orders obeyed, they consolidate what
they have won and then clean and administer
themselves. Once relieved and returned to
their own camps and lines again, they relax.
And as they sit round their camp fires in their
closely knit kin groups, so their broad smiles
return and teeth flash in the firelight as, with
an impish sense of fun, they recount the tales
that Gurkhas tell. In the cold and to restore
spirits at the end of an exacting day, tots of
rum may be passed around. Demanding little
from life, these brave and most natural of
fighting men will then, with the next day's
orders clear in their uncomplicated minds,
sleep until the next dawn, the next reveille
and the next call to duty.

Above: Sunrise
behind a Gurkha
roadblock sentry,
Cyprus 1974.
Left: With a
scarf about his
head against the
morning cold, an
old soldier
dreams his
dreams.

SERVICE WITH GURKHAS

S ERVICE WITH GURKHAS is a spiritual experience. It becomes a way of life so that one is utterly dedicated and totally involved. One is wedded to the unit, the unit is one's home and each Gurkha is a son to be cared for.

Across the very deep gulf of differences that separate them, the British officer and his men are attracted to one another and are drawn together. Their physical characteristics, whole life experience, social attitudes, thought processes, religion, beliefs and their mental and philosophical approach to life and its problems are so very different that out of the differences is born deep mutual respect of the hill Gurkha for his officer and of the officer for all his men. In short, the chemistry is correct.

The officer is the driving power of the unit. He provides the energy that drives the unit and gives it both a tight programme and difficult and demanding things to achieve so that it can have stature and pride and confidence in itself. Serving with Gurkhas essentially means sharing in all their experiences and shared experiences are the

very cement that binds a unit together and the tougher the shared experiences the firmer and more enduring will be the bonds between men and the stronger and more cohesive will the unit be, capable of withstanding much shock even if put under great pressure.

One gains so much from service with the enduring, uncomplaining and stolid Gurkha. He gives joy to people just by being what he is. The Gurkhas, by their simplicity and love for the simple things in life; by their infectious happiness and good humour; by their absurd sense of fun (that seeks out the ridiculous in life); by their ability to be buoyant despite great personal losses and severe hardships; by their great generosity, compassion and loyalty, teach one much. One learns to reorientate one's own sense of values and to appreciate more fully what are the things in life that really matter. A Gurkha teaches one the priceless assets of friends and friendship and the great importance of how to recognize and be happy with the good things in life: meals shared round a fire with the day's toil at an end; a drink by a stream of ice-cold mountain water on the long pull uphill; a simple picnic far from the hustle and bustle of life; how to relax free from materialism and the trivialities of life. They make you able to laugh at yourself, teach you about life and about yourself and they sweep you along by their happy, generous natures.

Leadership in a Gurkha unit has three elements: energy (applied by the leader), love (of the leader for his men and vice versa) and success (that the leader must provide.) So long as your men know you love and care for them and give them fair and strong leadership, then they will forgive you all your shortcomings and all your mistakes will be seen as having been deliberate.

Certainly, out of successful service with Gurkhas comes great affection so that on the day of departure when the officer must leave his unit for the last time, he will be unable to speak as he grasps the roughened hands of his men in silent farewells. And, when service with them must end, they will provide you with a host of wonderful memories that will buoy you up and carry you forward into the future, utterly content with the past and that you spent at least part of your life in the service of these brave hillmen of Nepal.

'Kaphar hunu bhanda mornu ramro'. 'It is better to die than to be a coward'. Old Gurkha proverb.

Inset: Felt hat and khukuri: emblems of the Gurkha as a fighting man.

'Gurkhali ayo!'
'The Gurkhas are upon you!'
Battle cry of the Gurkhas
down the ages.

the Gurkha Soldier

When the Great One made the Gurkha he must have had in mind His ideal
sort of human being, an elite among mankind . . .

For He took a hunk of cheerfulness
And gave it kind dark eyes
And bestowed upon it bravery
Far beyond its size.

To a body short in stature,
Of black hair and wheaten skin,
Were mixed in lots of gentleness
And a flashing, white-toothed grin.

Reliability, determination, honesty,
And a wee bit anger too,
Were deftly added by the Lord
And carefully kneaded through.

Made most generous of all men,
With the manners of a king,
Also made the happy warrior
With a love to dance and sing.

Straightforward and uninhibited
From a mountain way of life,
Patient, loyal and uncomplaining,
Inured to pain and strife.

Made proud and independent
By his Maker up above,
In battle bold and doughty,
In peace, goodwill and love.

With little in his pocket,
And but a small house on the ground,
No man is ever turned away,
No shelter left unfound.

Of different tribal habits,
Of varied jat and clan,
They all have this in common —
God's perfect gentleman.

———

The high mountains that begat him
Give him noble, kindly thoughts,
And the rivers that he ran by
Have cool secluded spots.

From a small white-washed homestead
With grey thatch above the eaves,
He tended young in distant pen
And bound the barley sheaves.

From mud-smoothed porch he looked afar,
Across rice valleys at his feet,
And to the north the mountains lay,
Cloud-bannered, snow and sleet.

From early youth he's carried loads,
A headband on his brow,
He helped his father build the fields
And fought behind the plough.

Steep mountain paths his legs have trod,
His naked limbs the trail,
Suns and winds have scorched him,
He's been lashed by rain and hail.

The mustard fields were yellow now,
And oranges were sweet,
As he left to be recruited
And strange new worlds to meet.

"Be faithful, Boy!" His father cried.
"Remember your good name.
 If needs must . . . you'll have to die.
 We don't have cowards but fame."

———————

Understanding 'faith' and 'honour'
And 'the regimental name',
He'll stick by task and comrade,
His code he will not shame.

He's sweated in the jungles,
There a perfect fighting man,
And shivering in trenches, waited,
Whilst those about him broke and ran.

When the rain comes down in torrents
And the wind permits no lee,
He'll make a fire from nothing
And all shall have sweet tea.

When time is hard to come by,
And the battle not yet won,
Shirt off, he's there before you
And the job is all but done.

When it's cold and damp foreboding
And the wind an icy stealth,
He'll flash a grin in your direction . . .
And the world will right itself.

Proud little Mountain Man,
Self-confident and true,
When others lie demoralized
He'll stand, saluting you.

And when the whole thing's o'er,
And Death does seek him out,
He'll go with calm and dignity,
He will not cry nor shout.

When bullets strike him down,
He'll fall but will not moan,
And the Lord will tug the top-knot
As He gathers to his own.

THIS BOOK is dedicated to Nepal and its brave people. In particular it is dedicated to the Gurkha hill soldier whose loyalty, bravery and fighting spirit are etched in tablets of stone across many continents but never more deeply than in the hearts of men who served with them, knew their friendship, experienced their generosity and were their proud commanders.

The hill Gurkha: Gangabahadur Gurung. His home is in a mountain village high in W. Nepal.

What is a Gurkha?

'Gurkha' refers to men of the martial hill tribes of Nepal and essentially to members of these tribes once they are recruited into military service. The word may have been derived from the name of the small township of Gorkha situated some 40 miles west of Kathmandu. It was in a hill castle perched on a small hilltop in Gorkha that the warlord Prithwi Narayan Shah, The Great, was born about the middle of the 18th century. He was to unify the many small warring tribal kingdoms of Nepal into one country and so, today, Gorkha is seen as both the symbol and the source of Nepalese unification and nationality.

Spread: The sun-flushed summits of Annapurna I (left, rear) and Annapurna South (centre). The black tip of the Fang is on the right. It is late evening and the jet winds are trailing banner clouds from off the summits.

Outside Front Cover: A Magar youth wrapped in the warm folds of his blanket. It is sunrise and the sun streams into the hill porch of his mountain home.

Outside Back Cover: A Gurkha sentry keeping the peace. Cyprus 1974.

Photography: All photographs in the book with the exception of the author's portrait on the inside back cover were taken by the author using Leica and Canon cameras loaded with Kodachrome film. No filters or artificial light sources were used.